The Best of Friends

Happy House

About Wise & Wide

- A systematic 6-level English reading program based on Lexile® measures
- Diverse and interesting topics chosen from the elementary curriculums of Korea and English speaking western countries
- Well-written books in various forms including fiction stories, descriptive texts, and classics retold
- The informative but original fiction stories grab your interest, leading to the easy and clear understanding of the educational content.
- Improve thinking skills with solid after-reading activities at all levels of the series.

Wise & Wide is a 6-level English reading program that consists of 60 books and each level is systematically divided by Lexile® measures. The Lexile® Framework for Reading is the most popular reading measuring system in American formal education curriculums and many English programs. Over 20 out of 50 states in the U.S. mark Lexile® measures directly on students' final report cards and over 300 well-known publishers adopt and use Lexile® measures.

Experience many kinds of readings written by professional writers from the U.S. and England. They used interesting topics that were carefully chosen after analyzing elementary curriculums from around the world including Korea, the U.S., England, and Australia among many others. Comprehensive after-reading activities including graphic organizers, speaking tasks, and After-reading Tests are ready for you.

Levels in the series and their corresponding Lexile® measures

Level	Lexile® measures	U.S. Grade
Level 1	Below 200L	Pre K - K
Level 2	190L - 400L	Lower Grade 1
Level 3	350L - 530L	Upper Grade 1
Level 4	420L - 650L	Grade 2
Level 5	520L - 940L	Grade 3 - 4
Level 6	830L - 1070L	Grade 5 - 6

* Smart Readers: Wise & Wide level 1 is applicable to the preschool level in the U.S.
* The source of the relationship between Lexile® measures and U.S. school grades: CCSS(Common Core State Standards) FOR ENGLISH LANGUAGE ARTS, APPENDIX A (2012, which is used by 45 states in the U.S.)

Topic List

	Level 1	Level 2	Level 3	Level 4	Level 5	Level 6
Book 1	Science>Biology: The hibernation of animals Story	Science>Biology: Living and nonliving things Story	Science>Biology> Animals & the Environment: Sea otters Story	Environment> Living with nature: The diver & the persimmon tree Story	Science>Biology> Animal: Amazing animals of the Amazon Story	Science>Biology: Germs, transmitted diseases Story
Book 2	Literature> World classics: Aesop's fables Story	Literature> Traditional fairy tale: Old tales about stones Story	Social Studies> Economy: To run a business to make and save money Story	Science>Biology> Plants: Photosynthesis Story	Science>Earth science: Earth's layers,earthquakes, volcanoes, and earth's atmosphere Report	Mathematics> Sequence: The golden ratio & the Fibonacci sequence Story
Book 3	Science>Physics: How shadows are formed Story	Literature> World classics: Peter Pan Story	Science>Scientific technology: Nanobots Story	Literature>Myths: World's creation stories Story	Literature> Legend: The story of King Arthur Story	Literature>Myths: Constellation myths Story
Book 4	Literature> Traditional literature: The Talmud Story	Science>Biology> Animal: Polar bears Story	Science>Biology> Animal: Mountain gorillas Story	Social Studies> Cultural anthropology: Amazing ancient cultures of the world Story	Science> Earth science: Clouds and weather Story	Literature> Human & animals: The friendship between a girl and a horse Story
Book 5	Social Studies> Ethics: Rules in daily life Story	Science>Biology: The five senses Report	Social Studies> Cultural anthropology: Astonishing festivals Report	Art>Music: Stories from two operas Story	Social Studies> World culture & history: The Renaissance Story	Sports> Board sports: Surfing & snowboarding Story
Book 6	Social Studies> World geography & travel: Tourist attractions around the world Story	Science>Biology> Animal: Dinosaurs Story	Science> Astronomy: The solar system Story	Social Studies> People: Three great people who overcame hardships Story	Science>Scientific technology: The wonderful world of robots Report	Art>Music: Composers of the Romantic Era Report
Book 7	Science> Space science: The life of astronauts Report	Social Studies> Cultural anthropology: Mythological monsters from around the world Report	Mathematics> Elementary mathematics: Numbers, measurement, shapes and data Report	Science & Social Studies> Technology & culture: Inventions from around the world Report	Art>Works of art: Famous paintings Report	Social Studies> Human & animals: Animals in action for human Report
Book 8	Social Studies> Cultural anthropology: Various living cultures of the world Story	Art>Music: Instruments in the orchestra Story		Social Studies> History: The California Gold Rush Report	Social Studies & Science> Psychology: Psychology in everyday life Story	Literature> World classics: The Merchant of Venice Story
Book 9						
Book 10						

10 books in each level will be published.

How to Use
This Book

•Before Reading

You can easily find the topic and what kind of story you are about to read.

•The text

All the stories were written by professional writers from the U.S. and England, so you will read authentic and appropriate English sentences and expressions in every book in the series.

•Pop Quiz

Check out right away if you understand what you have just read by solving a pop quiz that checks your comprehension.

•Key Words

The key words and expressions on each page are listed for you to easily study them.

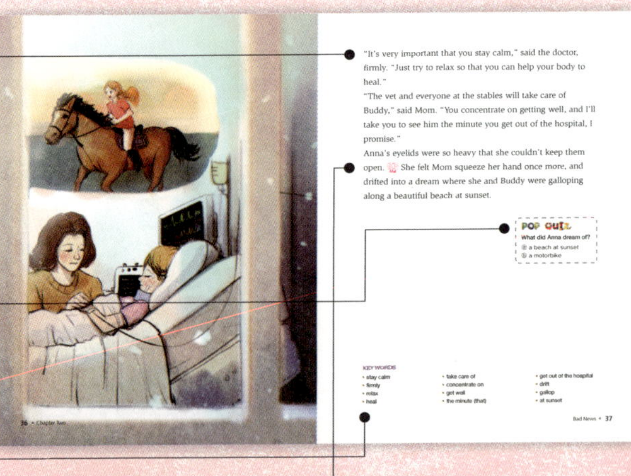

•Aha! Tips

Download free Korean explanations at *www.ihappyhouse.co.kr* for all of the sentences marked with "Aha!". These explain cultural, scientific, and economic knowledge or they deal with aspects of English such as grammatical structures or idiomatic expressions. There are lots of "Aha! Tips" to help you understand the text.

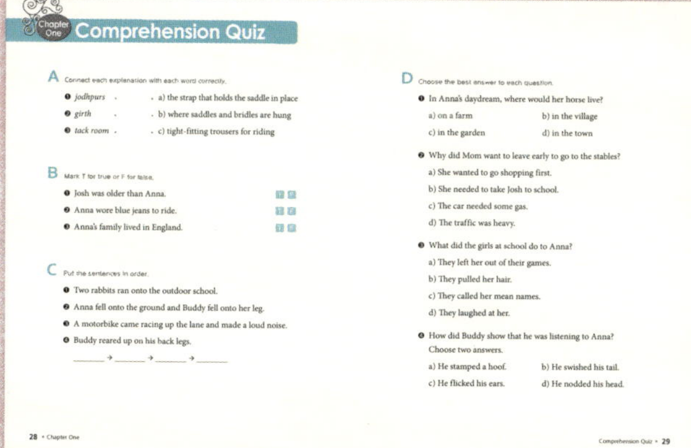

•Comprehension Quiz

After reading one chapter, solve various questions to find out if you fully understand the content.

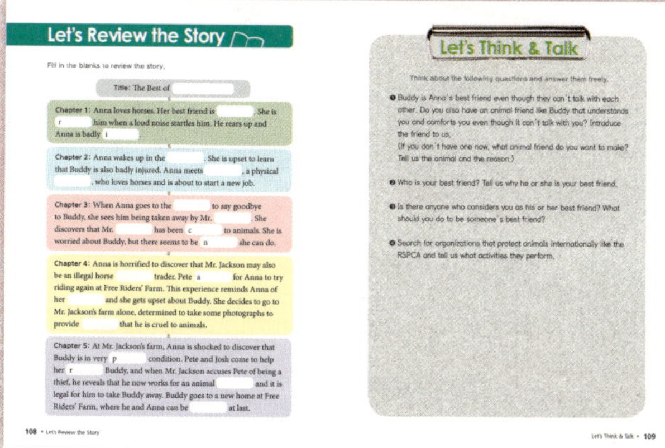

•Let's Review the Story /
•Let's Think & Talk

Fill in the blanks in the organizer to summarize the whole story. Express your own thinking and feelings about the story by answering the questions. You can build up logic and reasoning skills for your essay examinations in the future.

Appendix

Audio CD

In the CD audio book form, the texts are read vividly by American professional voice actors. (MP3 files downloaded for free)

After-reading Test

Solve an additionally provided After-reading Test for each book.

The Korean translation, Answer Keys, a Word Quiz, a Word List, and Aha! Tips for each book

You can download them for free at *www.ihappyhouse.co.kr* or *www.darakwon.co.kr*

Before Reading

The Best of Friends

A best friend who understands you

Who is your best friend? He or she could be your classmate or your sibling. But your best friend doesn't have to be a human. Some animals can be our best friends by being around us quietly and comforting us. People form friendships when they raise pets, showing affection to them, sharing joys and sorrows with them, and sometimes telling them their secrets. Having a special friendship with an animal has often been a theme for movies. *Free Willy* is a movie about the friendship between an Orca whale called Willy and a 12-year-old boy named Jesse. *Belle and Sebastien* is a movie about a 6-year-old shepherd boy and his dog Belle. Like these movies show, friendships with animals have the most beautiful, deepest and heart-felt feelings that you can have even though you are unable to talk with them.

Summary

Anna, a cheerful girl, always looks forward to taking her horseback riding class every week. Anna's best friend is a horse named Buddy that lives in the stables where she takes her class. Buddy is her best friend because she tells him all the bad things that happened at school and takes comfort from him! Therefore, she looks forward to the days when she can meet Buddy.

One day when there was a horseback riding class, Anna was practicing horseback riding with Buddy cheerfully. Suddenly, a motorbike came racing up the lane toward the stables and made a roaring sound. Startled by the sound, Buddy lost control and jumped up suddenly! Because of that, Anna and Buddy had a terrible accident...

Will Anna and Buddy be able to survive the ordeal and maintain their beautiful friendship for a long time?

Contents

The Best of Friends

The Best of Friends

From Dream to Disaster

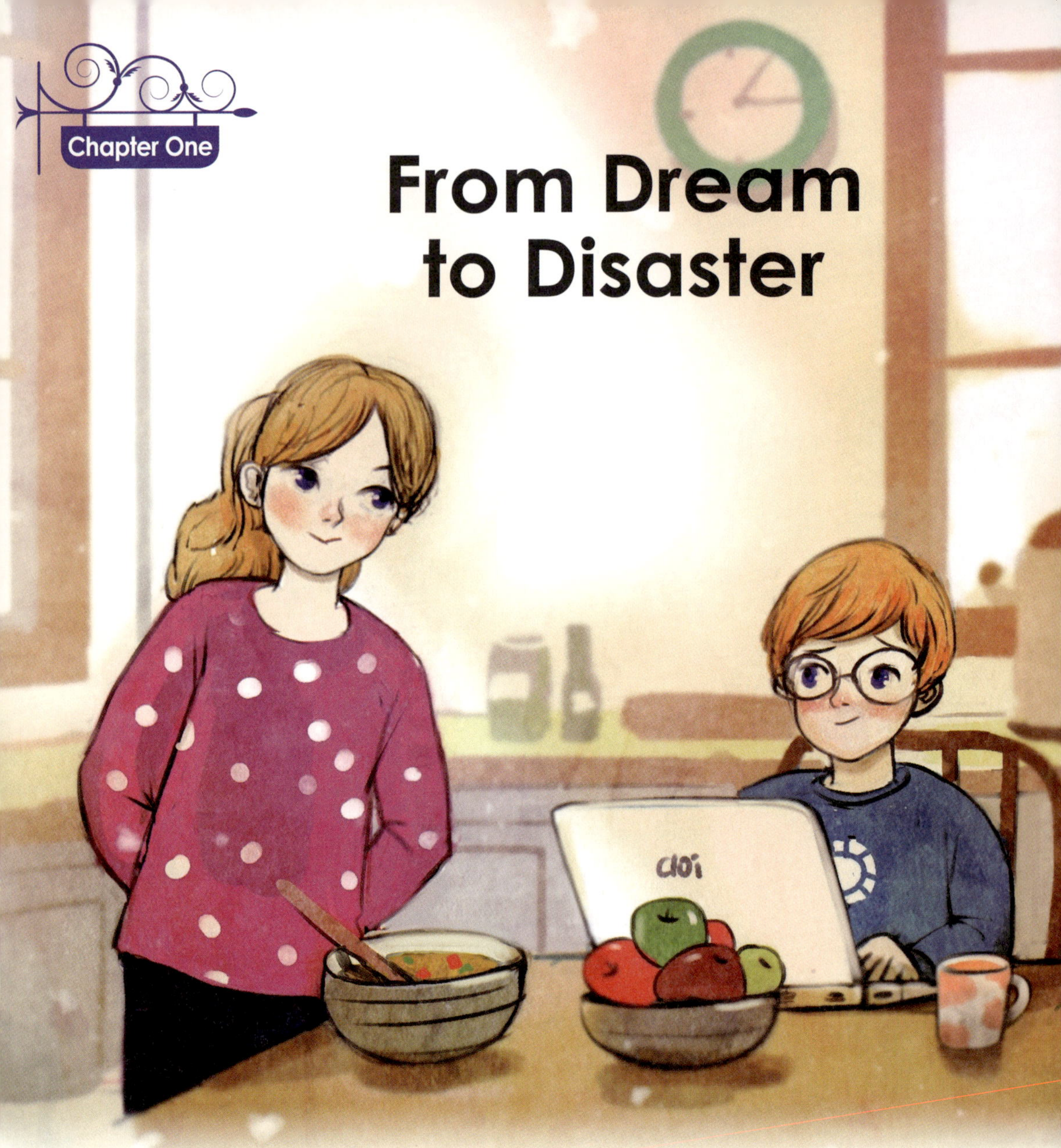

Anna looked at the clock and felt a surge of excitement in her stomach. "Only two hours and forty-two minutes until I can go riding again!" she announced, skipping around the kitchen.

Her younger brother, Josh, shook his head. "You've been talking about that just about every hour since you went to the stables *last* week. You're obsessed with those stupid horses."

"They're not stupid! You wouldn't understand, since *you're* obsessed with stupid computer games!"

"They're not as stupid as horses," shouted Josh. "At least computer games don't poop everywhere and make your clothes smell like a farmyard."

Anna snorted and stamped, very much like a horse herself. She loved the smell of her hands and her clothes after she'd been at the stables. How could Josh say that horses were stupid?

KEY WORDS

- disaster
- a surge of excitement (*cf*. surge)
- stomach
- go riding (go-went-gone)
- announce
- skip
- shake one's head (shake-shook-shaken)
- stable (*cf*. stables)

- be obsessed with (*cf*. obsess)
- understand
  (understand-understood-understood)
- at least
- poop
- farmyard
- snort
- stamp

Anna went to her bedroom and threw herself down on the bed, sighing. If only she had a horse of her own, then she wouldn't have to wait a whole week to go riding each time. She lay back and allowed herself to daydream for a while. She would get Dad to build a stable at the bottom of the garden, and her horse would live there.

Each morning, Anna would get up early and run down to greet it, and the horse would flick its ears back and forward, neighing gently to greet her. Then, she would put on its saddle and bridle, and the two of them would go for a long ride along the lanes and tracks near her country home. Where she lived, in an English village, lots of people had their own horses. Why should she be any different?

KEY WORDS

- **throw down** (throw-threw-thrown)
- **sigh**
- **if only**
- **lie back** (lie-lay-lain)
- **allow**
- **daydream**
- **for a while**
- **bottom**
- **greet**
- **flick**
- **forward**
- **neigh**

- **gently**
- **saddle**
- **bridle**
- **go for a ride** (cf. ride (ride-rode-ridden), rider)
- **lane**
- **track**
- **knock**
- **had better + *Verb***
- **get ready** (get-got-gotten)
- **heavy**
- **main road**
- **in time**

Just as Anna was planning exactly where she would ride,
there was a knock at the door that made her jump.

"Anna?" said Mom, opening the door. "You'd better start
getting ready. I heard that the traffic is very heavy on the
main road, so we'd better leave early to get to the stables in
time for your lesson."

Anna leaped up from the bed and went to her wardrobe to find her jodhpurs, the tight-fitting trousers that she wore especially for riding.

"Mom?" she said, just as Mom was leaving. "Why can't I have a horse of my own?"

Mom sighed. "You know why, Anna. We've talked about this so many times. We just can't afford to pay for a horse."

"But they're not that expensive," protested Anna.

"It's not just buying the horse," Mom went on, "but all the expense of looking after it."

She counted off on her fingers as she recited a list: "Food, vets' bills, a field, a stable, new shoes from the farrier every six weeks, a saddle and bridle… the list is endless!"

▲ a horseshoe(a piece of U-shaped metal that is attached to a horse's hoof)

KEY WORDS

- **leap up** (*cf.* leap)
- **wardrobe**
- **jodhpurs**
- **tight-fitting** (*cf.* tight)
- **trousers**
- **wear** (wear - wore - worn)
- **afford**

- **pay for**
- **protest**
- **go on**
- **expense**
- **look after**
- **count off on one's fingers**
- **recite**

- **vet**
- **bill**
- **field**
- **shoe**
- **farrier**
- **endless**

Anna knew that it was true, and she felt ashamed for asking again when Mom and Dad struggled to pay for the riding lessons each week.

"I'm sorry, honey," said Mom, resting a hand on Anna's shoulder, "but at least you've got your riding lesson to look forward to. Buddy will be excited to see you!"

Anna smiled at the thought of Buddy, and hurried to put on her jodhpurs.

KEY WORDS

- ashamed
- struggle
- rest
- look forward to
- excited
- hurry

The lane leading to the stables was rough, and the car jolted from side to side.

Anna gripped her riding helmet tightly and looked eagerly over the fence into the field. She could see the huge rectangular area called the outdoor school, where she and the other pupils would have their lesson.

This was the moment that she had been waiting for all week. 📖 Even before the car stopped in the stable yard, she had opened the door and unfastened her seat belt.

"Anna, wait!" said Mom. "There's no hurry to…"

KEY WORDS

- **lead** (lead-led-led)
- **jolt**
- **from side to side**
- **grip**
- **eagerly**
- **rectangular**

- **outdoor** (↔ indoor)
- **pupil**
- **unfasten**
- **seat belt**
- **race**
- **tack room**

- **block**
- **rush**
- **hang** (hang-hung-hung)
- **in neat rows**

But Anna had already jumped out of the car and was racing over to the small room, called the tack room, at the end of the stable block.

"Bye, Mom!" she called over her shoulder. "I'll see you in an hour."

She rushed into the tack room, where saddles and bridles were hanging in neat rows.

The riding instructor, Sally, was there, standing in front of a group of children and reading notes on a clipboard.

"James, you're going to ride Rocky today," she said, looking at a ginger-haired boy, "and Anna…" She looked up and smiled. "You're going to ride Buddy!"

Anna's grin almost split her face in two as she lifted a bridle from the hook marked "Buddy," and put his heavy saddle over her arm.

Of course she was riding Buddy. She always rode Buddy, because Buddy was her best friend in the world. He was the same age as her — twelve years old — but in the horse world that meant that he was an adult.

When the girls at school were mean and left her out of their games, she came to tell Buddy about it. He listened, flicking his ears backward and forward and nodding wisely, as she leaned against his warm, soft neck and poured out all her troubles. 🌐 Yes, she and Buddy really were the best of friends.

Now his head appeared over the stable door and he neighed in greeting. His coat was a beautiful rich brown, and his long black mane flopped over his neck.

KEY WORDS

- instructor
- clipboard
- ginger-haired
- grin
- split (split-split-split)
- hook
- of course

- mean (mean-meant-meant)
- adult
- leave out of (leave-left-left)
- backward (↔ forward)
- nod
- wisely
- lean against

- pour out
- appear
- coat
- rich
- mane
- flop

Anna opened the stable door and slipped in beside him, inhaling the rich scents of hay and warm horse. She slid the saddle onto his back and put on the bridle, the heavy metal bit slipping comfortably into his mouth.

"Are you ready to go, Buddy?" she whispered, leading him out into the yard.

She checked that the girth — the long strap that went round Buddy's body and held the saddle in place — was tight enough, placed her left foot into the stirrup and swung herself up into the saddle.

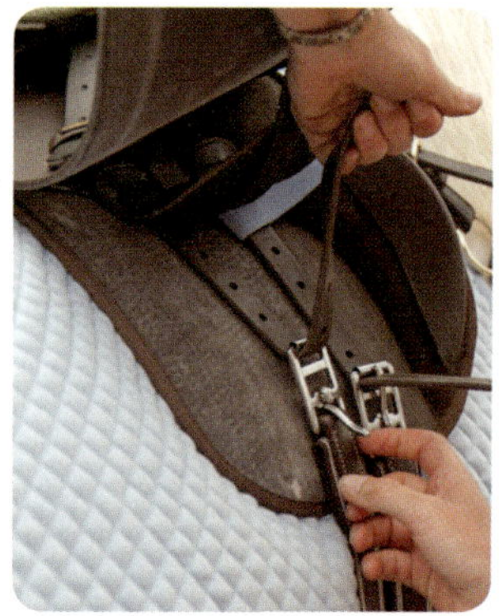

▲ tightening the girth on the saddle

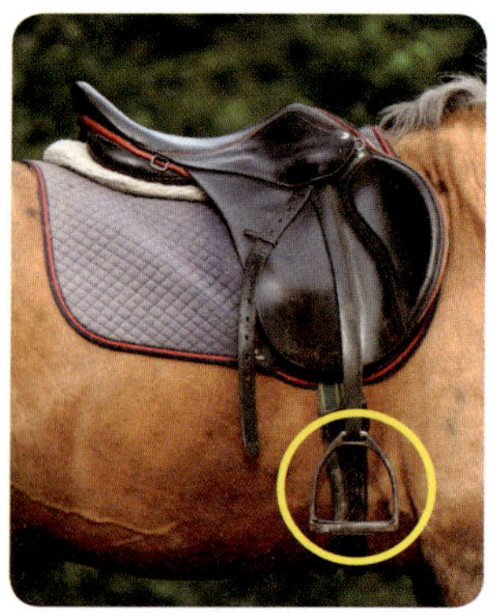

▲ a saddle with stirrups

KEY WORDS

- **slip in** (*cf.* slip)
- **inhale**
- **scent**
- **hay**
- **slide** (slide-slid-slid)
- **bit**
- **comfortably**
- **whisper**
- **girth**
- **strap**
- **go round**
- **in place** (*cf.* place)
- **enough**
- **stirrup**
- **swing** (swing-swung-swung)

Anna gathered the reins into her hands and squeezed her legs to let him know that it was time to walk.  Then, the two of them made their way to the outdoor school for their lesson.

There were eight children in the group, some of them relaxed and confident and one or two a little nervous. The instructor, Sally, ordered them to ride around the outside edge of the school while she stood in the middle and watched them closely.

"James, sit up straighter," she called. "Catherine, press your heels down."

KEY WORDS

- gather
- rein
- squeeze
- make one's way

- relaxed (*cf.* relax)
- confident
- nervous
- order

- edge
- straighter
- press down (*cf.* press)
- heel

Anna listened to the instructions and made sure that she was doing all the right things. A slight pressure on the left rein made Buddy turn to the left. She found it amazing that she could communicate with him by such simple actions.

"Anna, please take Buddy forward into a trot," called Sally. Anna shortened the reins, sat down deep into the saddle and squeezed both legs at the same time. Buddy responded by breaking into a trot, and Anna's body rose gently up and down with each stride.

"Good boy, Buddy," she said, and he trotted faster.

"Okay, Anna, let's see Buddy cantering round the school please," said Sally.

Anna pressed her lips together as she remembered all the things she had to do in order to tell Buddy what was happening next. She stopped rising up and down, and sat down in the saddle, bumping around a little bit. She squeezed both legs harder against his sides, her left leg pressing on the girth and her right leg a little further back. This made Buddy begin to canter around in a counter-clockwise direction.

Anna relaxed, enjoying the rocking motion… and that was when it happened.

POP QUIZ

How did Anna tell Buddy to walk forward?
ⓐ She squeezed him with her legs.
ⓑ She shook the reins.

KEY WORDS

- **instruction**
- **make sure**
- **slight**
- **communicate with**
- **trot**
- **shorten**
- **at the same time**
- **respond**
- **break into** (break-broke-broken)

- **rise** (rise-rose-risen)
- **stride** (stride-strode-stridden)
- **canter**
- **in order to** + *Verb*
- **bump**
- **a little bit**
- **further**
- **counter-clockwise direction**
- **rocking**

A motorbike came racing up the lane toward the stables, the engine roaring. Startled, Buddy swerved to one side.

"It's all right, Buddy," murmured Anna, only just managing to stay in the saddle.

All of a sudden, the motorbike's exhaust pipe gave a loud bang like a gunshot. A couple of rabbits, which had been sitting quietly by the fence, eating grass, ran out onto the outdoor school and dashed in front of Buddy's hooves.

He reared up on his back legs, higher and higher, while Anna held onto his black mane and the front of the saddle. She tried her hardest to hold on, but her feet slipped out of the stirrups and she fell backward, hitting the ground hard.

KEY WORDS

- race up
- roar
- startled
- swerve to
- murmur
- only just
- manage
- all of a sudden
- exhaust pipe
- bang
- gunshot
- dash
- hooves
- rear
- hold onto (hold-held-held)
- try one's hardest[best]

Buddy seemed to stand up for a long moment, and then his back twisted and he fell sideways, right onto the spot where Anna had fallen.

She tried to roll out of the way, but her body didn't seem to work properly. All the breath had been knocked out of her lungs, and she felt dizzy.

"Buddy…" she gasped as he crashed down onto her left leg, and a pain like fiery needles shot through her body. Buddy's hooves churned up the grass and mud as he struggled to get up.

The last thing she saw was Buddy collapsing onto his side, snorting in pain as his legs twisted beneath him. And then everything went black.

KEY WORDS

- seem
- twist
- sideways
- spot
- roll
- out of the way
- properly

- breath (*cf.* breathe)
- knock out of
- lung
- dizzy
- gasp
- crash down
- fiery

- shoot (shoot-shot-shot)
- churn
- collapse
- beneath
- go black

A Connect each explanation with each word correctly.

❶ *jodhpurs* .　　　. a) the strap that holds the saddle in place

❷ *girth* .　　　. b) where saddles and bridles are hung

❸ *tack room* .　　　. c) tight-fitting trousers for riding

B Mark T for true or F for false.

❶ Josh was older than Anna.　　　T　F

❷ Anna wore blue jeans to ride.　　　T　F

❸ Anna's family lived in England.　　　T　F

C Put the sentences in order.

❶ Two rabbits ran onto the outdoor school.

❷ Anna fell onto the ground and Buddy fell onto her leg.

❸ A motorbike came racing up the lane and made a loud noise.

❹ Buddy reared up on his back legs.

________ → ________ → ________ → ________

 Choose the best answer to each question.

❶ In Anna's daydream, where would her horse live?

a) on a farm   b) in the village

c) in the garden   d) in the town

❷ Why did Mom want to leave early to go to the stables?

a) She wanted to go shopping first.

b) She needed to take Josh to school.

c) The car needed some gas.

d) The traffic was heavy.

❸ What did the girls at school do to Anna?

a) They left her out of their games.

b) They pulled her hair.

c) They called her mean names.

d) They laughed at her.

❹ How did Buddy show that he was listening to Anna?
Choose two answers.

a) He stamped a hoof.   b) He swished his tail.

c) He flicked his ears.   d) He nodded his head.

Chapter Two

Bad News

Everything in Anna's body hurt. Even before she opened her eyes, she knew that something was very wrong. She could hear someone crying beside her bed, sobbing in great gulps and gasping her name.

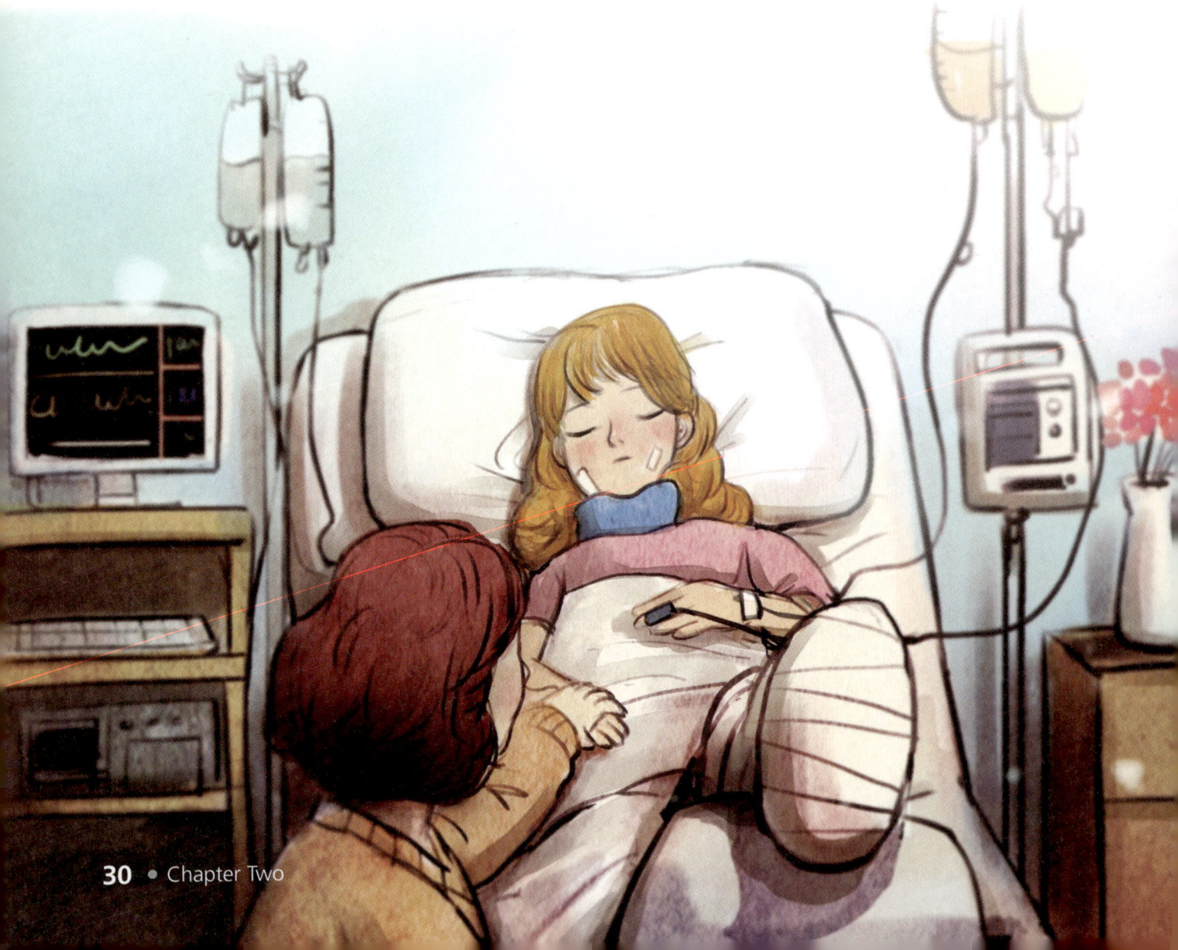

Anna tried to open her eyes and to move her body, but everything felt so heavy and painful. She could feel a hand wrapped around hers, the fingers squeezing and rubbing. Anna wanted to squeeze back, but she couldn't make her fingers work properly.

At last, she managed a tiny squeeze of her fingers, and her eyelids flickered open for an instant before falling closed again.

There was a shriek from the person beside her, and now she recognized Mom's voice.

"Nurse!" Mom shouted. "Doctor! Someone come quickly! I think she's waking up!"

KEY WORDS

- **hurt** (hurt-hurt-hurt)
- **sob**
- **in a gulp**
- **painful**

- **wrap**
- **rub**
- **eyelid**
- **flicker**

- **for an instant**
- **shriek**
- **recognize**
- **wake up** (wake-woke-woken)

There was the sound of running feet and a bright light was shone onto Anna's eyes so that the insides of her eyelids looked red. Warm fingers lifted her eyelids for her and the light was shone quickly into one eye and then the other.

"Both the pupils in her eyes are responding to light as they should," said the doctor. "That tells us that there is no serious brain damage."

"Is she going to be all right?" That was Dad's voice.

Anna didn't know that he had been sitting there, too, but hearing his voice gave her even more determination to wake up properly. She managed to lift her arm briefly before it flopped back onto the bed, and when the doctor released her eyelids, she managed to open them herself.

Mom and Dad threw themselves on her, crying and hugging until the doctor reminded them to be careful.

"Your daughter has had a very serious accident," he said, "and it is going to take a long time for her to recover fully."

"But she *will* recover fully, won't she?" asked Dad.

The doctor hesitated before answering, his voice gentle and concerned. "We hope so, but her thigh bone was badly broken and there may be a lot of damage to the nerves in her left leg, which may make walking difficult. She will need weeks — or even months — of physical therapy."

KEY WORDS

- determination
- briefly
- release
- throw oneself
- remind

- be careful
- accident
- recover
- fully
- hesitate

- concerned
- thigh
- nerve
- physical therapy
  (*cf.* physical)

Anna opened her mouth to speak, but her throat felt as dry as the sawdust that she scattered on the floor of Buddy's stable. She coughed and choked a little before managing to say the one word that nobody was saying: "Buddy?"

At first, neither Mom nor Dad replied, but simply looked at one another as if they didn't understand the question.

So Anna said it again: "Buddy? Is he okay?"

Dad rested a hand on her shoulder and Mom took hold of Anna's hand again, shaking her head.

"I'm sorry, honey, but he was very badly injured too."

"The most important thing is that *you're* going to be all right," said Dad, briskly, "and worrying about some horse isn't going to help."

Buddy isn't just "some horse," thought Anna. *He's my best friend!*

KEY WORDS

- sawdust
- scatter
- cough
- choke
- neither A nor B

- simply
- one another
- as if
- take hold of
  (take-took-taken)

- injured
- briskly
- panic
- tighten
- beep

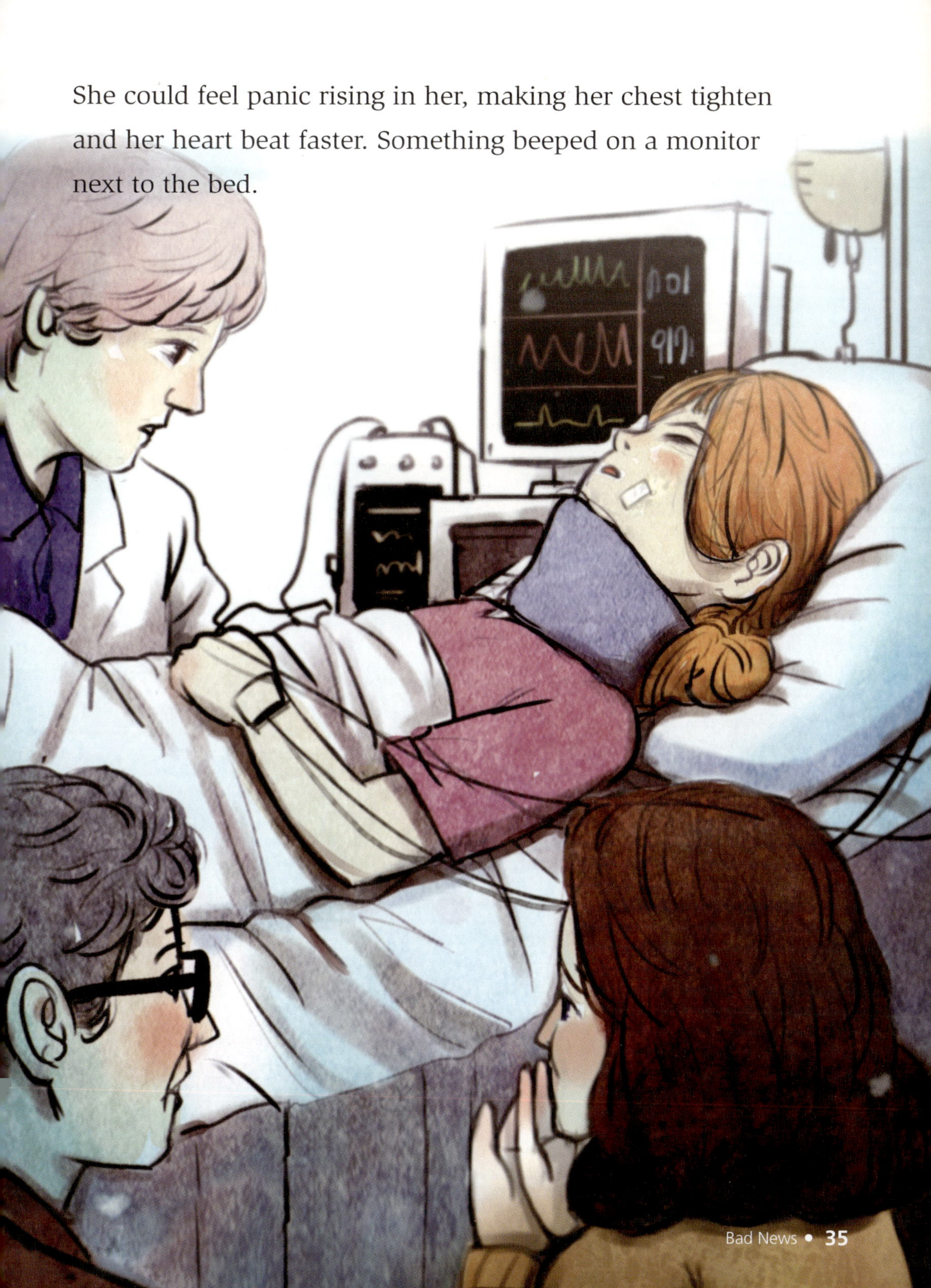

She could feel panic rising in her, making her chest tighten and her heart beat faster. Something beeped on a monitor next to the bed.

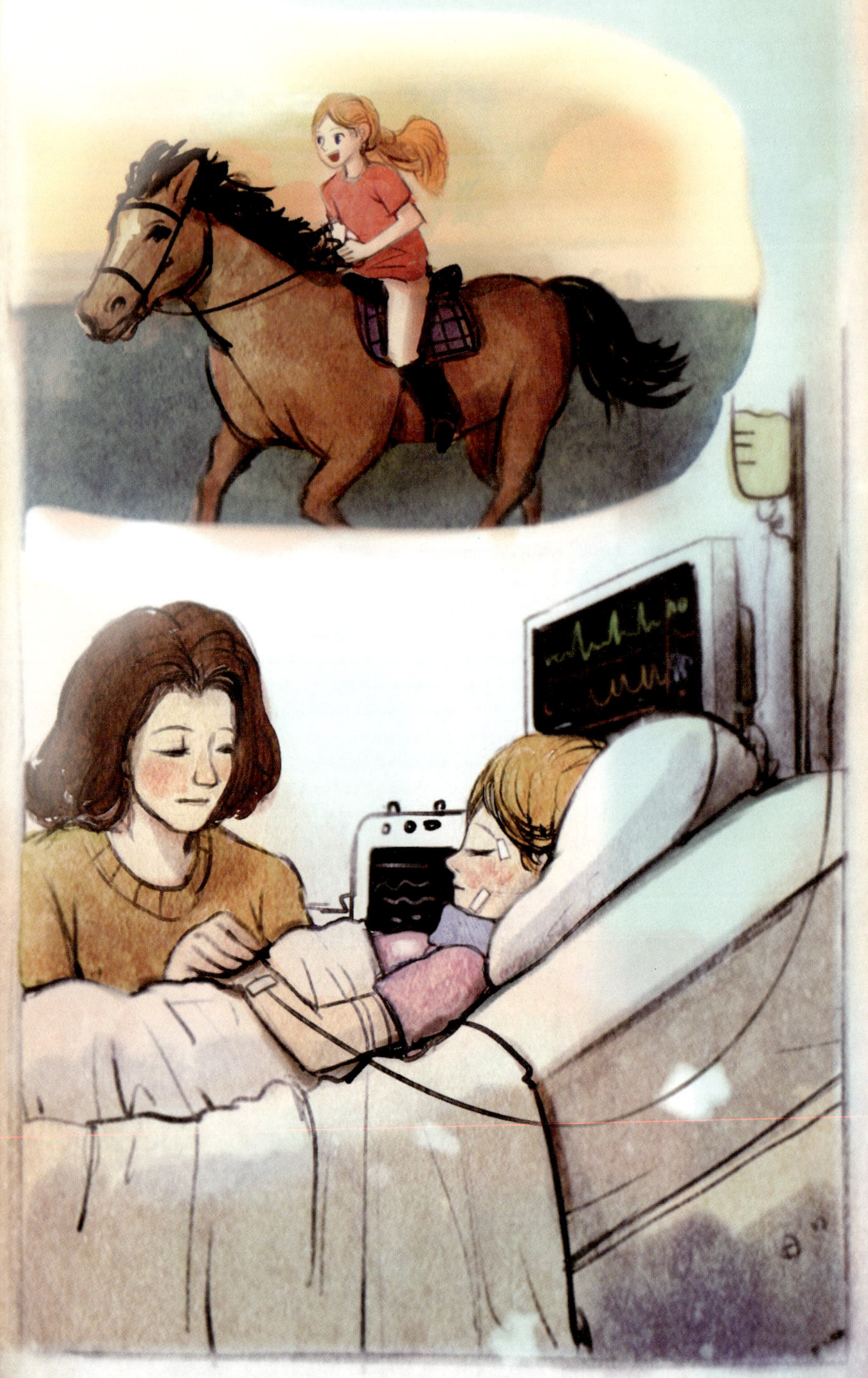

"It's very important that you stay calm," said the doctor, firmly. "Just try to relax so that you can help your body to heal."

"The vet and everyone at the stables will take care of Buddy," said Mom. "You concentrate on getting well, and I'll take you to see him the minute you get out of the hospital, I promise."

Anna's eyelids were so heavy that she couldn't keep them open.  She felt Mom squeeze her hand once more, and drifted into a dream where she and Buddy were galloping along a beautiful beach at sunset.

KEY WORDS

- stay calm
- firmly
- relax
- heal

- take care of
- concentrate on
- get well
- the minute (that)

- get out of the hospital
- drift
- gallop
- at sunset

It was a long and difficult month in the hospital for Anna.
The physical therapist, Pete, came each day to massage
Anna's right leg and to help her muscles work again.
Pete was a tall, broad, muscular man with black hair who
looked quite strict, but whose touch on her skin was warm
and gentle.
Anna's left leg was encased in a hard white plaster cast,
which made her skin itch beneath it.

"We'll soon have you out of bed," said Pete, as he helped her to exercise the leg that wasn't in a plaster cast. "We just need to build up the muscles in this leg first. They soon get weak if you stay in bed for a long time."

Mom and Dad came to visit each day, sometimes bringing Josh after school. But all Anna could think about was Buddy.

"How's he doing?" she asked Mom every day, and every day Mom said, "Don't worry about Buddy. I'm sure he's doing fine."

"Have you been to the stables to see him?" asked Anna.

"No, of course I haven't," said Mom, wearily, "because I come to the hospital to see *you* instead."

And so the weeks went by, with Anna getting stronger each day.

KEY WORDS

- physical therapist
- muscle
- broad
- muscular
- strict

- encase
- plaster cast
- itch
- **build up** (build-built-built)
- sometimes

- wearily
- instead
- go by

"I've never seen anyone so determined to get back on their feet," laughed Pete as he helped her in and out of a wheelchair. "Is there somewhere else you have to be?"
"Yes," said Anna, as she struggled to move her leg. "My friend Buddy needs me, because he was in the accident too."
Pete frowned and said, "Is he in this hospital somewhere?"

Anna managed a small smile at the thought of Buddy lying
in a hospital bed, making the sheets all dirty with his hooves.
"He's a horse," she said.

"I love horses," said Pete. "I used to have my own when I
was a boy, back in New Zealand. I'd like to have one again;
perhaps I will when I start my new job."

"New job? Does that mean you're leaving here?" asked Anna.
Pete nodded his head. "But it starts in a few weeks, so I'll be
here to help you to get better first!"

Anna wanted to ask him more about the new job, but she
didn't have the energy. Instead, she gritted her teeth against
the pain and continued with her exercises.

KEY WORDS

- determined
- get back on one's feet
- wheelchair
- frown
- at the thought of
- lying
- sheet
- used to + *Verb*
- would like to + *Verb*
- perhaps
- grit one's teeth
- continue with

At last, the day came when Anna was released from the hospital. Mom and Dad came to collect her in the car.

"Let's take you home," said Dad, with a sigh of relief.

"I don't want to go home yet," said Anna. "I want to go to the stables and see Buddy first."

"You can't go there now," said Dad, frowning. "We need to get you straight home so you can rest."

"But Mom promised that we could," said Anna.

Mom sighed, shrugged her shoulders and said, "I did promise, but… it's not good news, honey. I called the stables this morning to let them know that you were coming out of the hospital and they said that…"

Her voice trailed off, as though she didn't want to say any more.

"What did they say?" demanded Anna.

"They said that they can't afford to pay the vet's bills for Buddy anymore, so they will have to sell him. His leg is too badly injured, and it would cost thousands of pounds to fix it. You know that they don't have much money there."

Anna knew that horses were expensive to keep, and that the people who owned the stables were always short of money.  Her throat felt tight, as though there was a big lump in it. She couldn't stop the tears that spilled from her eyes onto her cheeks.

If only that motorbike hadn't come along the lane at that moment, then everything would be different now, she thought.

It was frightening the way that everything could change in a single moment.

"Can I go and see him?" she whispered. "If he's going somewhere else, then I just want to… say… goodbye."

What did Anna find frightening?

ⓐ the thought of riding again
ⓑ the way that everything could change in a moment

KEY WORDS

- be short of money
- lump

- spill
- frightening

Chapter Two Comprehension Quiz

A Match each line with the right character.

- ❶
- ❷
- ❸
- ❹

- a) "It's not good news, honey."
- b) "We'll soon have you out of bed."
- c) "But she will recover fully, won't she?"
- d) "Does that mean you're leaving here?"

B Mark T for true or F for false.

❶ When Anna woke up, she began to cry.   T   F

❷ When Anna woke up, she could feel someone holding her hand.   T   F

❸ When Anna woke up, Josh was there.   T   F

❹ When Anna woke up, her left leg was broken.   T   F

C Choose the best answer to each question.

❶ Why was Anna so determined to get back on her feet quickly?

a) She wanted to see Buddy.

b) She wanted to please her parents.

c) She wanted to go back to school.

d) She wanted to impress Pete.

❷ Why didn't Anna ask Pete more about his new job?

a) She did not know that he was leaving.

b) She did not have enough energy.

c) She did not want him to leave.

d) She did not speak the same language as he did.

D Circle the right word(s) for each underlined part.

❶ At last, the day came when Anna was (barred / escaped / released) from the hospital.

❷ It would (cost / win / save) thousands of pounds to fix Buddy's injured leg.

❸ Anna wanted to see Buddy in order to say (hello / get well / goodbye).

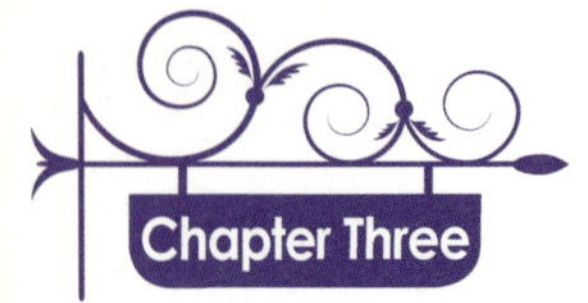

Heading into Danger

The lane leading to the stables was as rough as ever, but
Anna was determined not to let her parents see how much
the journey hurt her.

When they pulled into the stable yard, an unfamiliar truck
was parked there, the back door open.

A wooden ramp led into the dark interior of the truck, and a
man stood next to it, his face twisted with impatience.

He was smoking a cigarette, and Anna wrinkled her nose at
the smell as Mom opened the car door and helped her out.

He should know that it was dangerous to smoke near hay
and straw. She wondered what he was doing here.

KEY WORDS

- head
- as ~ as ever
- journey
- pull into
- unfamiliar (↔ familiar)

- park
- wooden
- ramp
- interior
- impatience

- smoke
- cigarette
- wrinkle
- straw
- wonder

T. JACKSON &

A minute later, Anna had her answer.

Sally, the riding instructor, came out of one of the stables, her head down, a rope in her hand. The other end of the rope was attached to Buddy's head collar.

He followed Sally with his head down, and he walked terribly slowly, limping heavily. One of his hind legs was bandaged and there was a streak of dried blood on it.

"Buddy?" Anna wanted to run to him, but all she could do was to lean on Mom while Dad hurried round to the trunk to get the wheelchair out.

At the sound of her voice, Buddy lifted his head, but the effort seemed to be too much, and he dropped it again.

KEY WORDS

- the other
- be attached to
- head collar
- follow
- terribly

- limp
- heavily
- hind leg
- bandage
- streak

- trunk
- effort
- be too much

"Oh, Buddy," whispered Anna, her hands reaching for him. Dad pushed her closer and Sally stood still, giving Anna time to run her hands through Buddy's black mane and to stroke his beautiful face.

He dropped his soft muzzle trustingly into the palm of her hand, and Anna pressed her forehead against the white star between his eyes.

KEY WORDS

- reach for
- still
- run one's hand through
- stroke 
- muzzle
- trustingly 
- palm

"Where is he going?" she asked.

"I'm so sorry, Anna," said Sally, barely able to speak. "We had no choice but to sell him. That man over there by the trailer is a friend of the stable owner's cousin. He offered to buy Buddy."

"Why would he buy a horse that can't walk properly?" Anna watched the man throw his cigarette butt onto the ground and press it with the sole of his boot to make sure it was out.

"He says that he has a retired racehorse and it's alone in the field, so it needs a companion."

Perhaps things will be okay after all, thought Anna.

She would miss Buddy terribly, but she imagined him grazing under a tree in a field full of green grass with an old horse for company, his leg healing in the sunshine.

She kissed him on the forehead and whispered, "Goodbye, Buddy. I'll find out where you are and I'll come to visit you."

KEY WORDS

- barely
- be able to + *Verb* (= can)
- have no choice but to + *Verb*
- trailer
- offer

- butt
- sole
- out
- retired
- racehorse

- companion
- after all
- graze
- full of
- for company

J. JACKSON

Dad pulled the wheelchair away and Anna watched as Sally led Buddy toward the ramp that led into the dark truck. Buddy hesitated on the ramp, his nostrils flaring wide and his ears flicking back and forward.

"Get in there, you stupid horse," snapped the man, smacking Buddy with his hand. Buddy's ears went flat against his neck to show that he was angry.

"Don't show me a pair of flat ears!" shouted the man as he went to the cab of the truck and took out a whip. "I'll use this on you to teach you a lesson!"

Anna wanted to jump out of her wheelchair and lead Buddy into the truck. She didn't like that man at all.

Fortunately, Sally managed to lead Buddy in and she tied him up next to a net full of hay.

Anna let out her breath and told herself that everything would be all right.

The man removed the ramp and closed the back door so that Anna couldn't see Buddy anymore. The engine started up, giving off a cloud of black smoke, and away it went, taking Buddy to his new home.

As the truck left, Anna read the name painted on the side — *J. Jackson & Co.* — and made sure that she remembered it.

POP QUIZ

How did Buddy show that he was angry?

ⓐ His nostrils flared wide.

ⓑ His ears went flat against his neck.

KEY WORDS

- pull away
- nostril
- flare
- snap
- smack
- flat

- cab
- whip
- teach a lesson
  (teach-taught-taught)
- at all
- fortunately

- let out (let-let-let)
- remove
- start up
- give off
- Co.

It was strange to be home again after so many weeks in the hospital.

It was impossible for Anna to walk up the stairs to her bedroom, so Dad had to carry her, just as he had done when she was a small child. He put her down on the bed and rubbed his aching back before kissing the top of her head.

"It's good to have you home," he said. "I'll just go down and help Mom to bring your things in from the car."

After Dad left, Anna looked around her bedroom, which was just as she had left it on that day when she had gone to the stables and the accident had happened.

The walls were covered with pictures and posters of horses and ponies of all shapes, sizes, and colors. But her most treasured possession was the photograph of Buddy in a silver frame next to her bed.

Where did Anna keep the photograph of Buddy?
ⓐ on a high shelf
ⓑ next to her bed

KEY WORDS

- impossible
- carry
- just as

- aching (*cf.* ache)
- be covered with
- picture (= photograph)

- pony
- treasured possession
- frame

She picked it up and looked into his deep brown eyes.
"I'll find out where you are," she promised, "and I'll do it now before I forget the name on the truck."

Anna knew that *Co.* meant "company," so the man must be J. Jackson and he must own some kind of business.

She picked up her tablet computer, typed *J. Jackson & Co.* into the search box, and waited for the browser to bring up the information she needed.

- **forget** (forget-forgot-forgotten)
- **must**
- **business**
- **tablet computer**
- **type**
- **search box** (*cf.* search)
- **browser**
- **bring up** (bring-brought-brought)

There was no official website for *J. Jackson & Co.* Instead, the search result showed a list of European meat companies. Perhaps Mr. Jackson was a sheep farmer, or a man who reared beef cattle on his farm.

She smiled as she pictured Buddy surrounded by lambs, skipping about in a field.

But then, Anna saw something that made her heart thud.

There was a link to a local newspaper article that had been written two years ago.

It said that Mr. Jackson had been accused of animal cruelty. He had kept some horses in such poor conditions that they were taken away from him and one of them later died. He was not allowed to keep animals for a whole year after that. And now this man had Buddy!

KEY WORDS

- official
- website
- result
- European
- sheep farmer
- rear
- beef cattle
- surrounded by
- lamb
- thud
- link
- local
- article
- be accused of
- cruelty
- take away from

Anna wanted to leap up from the bed and race down the stairs, but even a small movement sent pain shooting down her plastered leg.

How was she supposed to go and rescue Buddy when she couldn't even bear her own weight to walk across the room?

"Dad!" she yelled, her body tense with frustration and panic.

A door banged downstairs and hurried footsteps pounded up the stairs.

- plastered
- be supposed to + *Verb*
- rescue
- bear (bear-bore-born)
- yell
- tense
- frustration
- footstep

A moment later, Dad burst into the room, his face pale and anxious. "What is it, Anna? Are you all right?"

In that instant, she realized just how worried her parents had been all those weeks she had been in the hospital.

"Dad," she said, almost throwing the tablet at him, "you've got to take a look at this."

He frowned, and peered at the tablet over the top of his glasses to read the small print more easily.

"I don't understand," he said slowly. "Who — or what — is
J. Jackson & Co. and why are you so interested?"
"It's that man, Dad — the one who took Buddy away. He
treats his animals so badly that some of them die!"
"Anna," said Dad, "this is none of our business, you know.
Buddy doesn't belong to us, and we don't know that this
man will treat him badly. He told the stables that Buddy was
going to be a companion to a retired racehorse, so we can't
go there and call him a liar! He may have treated his animals
badly two years ago, but I'm sure that he's learned his lesson
now."

POP QUIZ

What made Anna realize how worried her parents
had been while she was in hospital?

ⓐ the fact that Dad carried her up the stairs
ⓑ the fact that Dad came up the stairs so quickly,
    looking anxious

KEY WORDS

- burst into
- pale
- anxious
- in that instant
- realize

- have got to + *Verb*
- take a look at
- peer at
- print
- interested

- treat
- none of our business
- belong to
- liar

"What about Sally?" asked Anna. "I'm sure she would help us if she knew what Mr. Jackson was really like."

"Sally is leaving her job at the stables," said Dad. "They can't afford to employ her because a lot of parents have taken their children out of their lessons since your accident."

Anna felt sorry for Sally. It seemed that so many people's lives had been affected by a single accident.

"But, Dad… we have to find out for sure!"

Anna knew that she couldn't do anything at all without her parents' help. She couldn't walk or cycle to Mr. Jackson's farm, even though the address was right there on the tablet. She couldn't even take the bus. How on earth could she get her wheelchair onto a bus?

Why couldn't Anna take the bus to Mr. Jackson's farm?

ⓐ It would be too difficult to get her wheelchair onto a bus.
ⓑ Anna had no money to pay the bus fare.

KEY WORDS

▪ leave one's job	▪ without	▪ sink (sink-sank-sunk)
▪ employ	▪ cycle	▪ focus on
▪ feel sorry for (feel-felt-felt)	▪ even though	▪ abandon
▪ affect	▪ address	▪ set (set-set-set)
▪ for sure	▪ how on earth	▪ in a straight line

Her heart sank as Dad shook his head. "You have to forget about Buddy and focus on getting yourself back to good health," he said.

"No, we can't just abandon him!" gasped Anna.

Dad stood up, his mouth set in a straight line. "I don't want to hear any more about this."

Chapter Three   Comprehension Quiz

 **A**   Mark T for true or F for false.

❶ The lane leading to the stables was very rough.   T   F

❷ When Anna arrived at the stables, the door of the truck was closed.   T   F

❸ Sally walked out of Buddy's stable with her head down.   T   F

❹ Buddy's front legs had a bandage on them.   T   F

B   Choose the best answer to each question.

❶ What did Anna smell when she stepped out of the car?

    a) hay and straw   b) horse poop

    c) gas from the truck   d) cigarette smoke

❷ Why did Mr. Jackson say that he wanted to buy Buddy?

    a) He wanted to teach Buddy new tricks.

    b) He wanted to use Buddy to teach children to ride.

    c) He wanted Buddy to be a companion for a retired racehorse.

    d) He wanted Buddy to be a pet for his cousin.

 Fill in each blank with the right word below to complete each sentence.

treasured	aching	poor	official

❶ Dad put Anna down on the bed and rubbed his ______________ back.

❷ Anna's most ______________ possession was the photograph of Buddy.

❸ There was no ______________ website for *J. Jackson & Co.*

❹ Mr. Jackson had kept animals in very ______________ conditions.

D Circle the right word for each underlined part.

❶ It was two (<u>weeks</u> / <u>years</u> / <u>months</u>) ago when Mr. Jackson was (<u>accused</u> / <u>arrested</u> / <u>annoyed</u>) of cruelty to animals.

❷ The stables could no longer (<u>employ</u> / <u>teach</u> / <u>treat</u>) Sally, so she had to find a new (<u>home</u> / <u>job</u> / <u>horse</u>).

❸ So many people's lives had been (<u>infected</u> / <u>affected</u> / <u>deflected</u>) by a single (<u>horse</u> / <u>accident</u> / <u>person</u>).

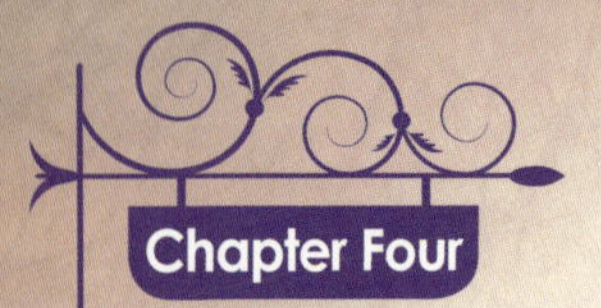

Push through the Fear

Each morning, Anna woke to two kinds of pain. The first
kind was physical, a dull ache in her left leg and a sharp pain
in the same hip, but the second kind of pain was worse. It
was the pain of knowing that Buddy might be suffering and
that she could do nothing at all to help him.

Each morning, Mom helped her to shower and dress, which
was embarrassing and made her feel like a little kid again.
Then, Dad carried her down the stairs and strapped her into
her wheelchair before leaving for work. He had to take the
bus, since Mom needed the car to drive Anna to the hospital
for her physical therapy with Pete.

The plaster cast had been removed now, but Anna's left leg
was still weak, the skin pale and dry.

POP QUIZ

According to the information in the text, match the two sides.

ⓐ Anna felt a sharp pain　　·　　　　·　① in her hip.

ⓑ Anna felt a dull ache　　·　　　　·　② in her left leg.

KEY WORDS

- a dull ache
- worse
- suffer
- embarrassing
- leave for work

"What's happened to you?" Pete asked, as Anna went through all her exercises without enthusiasm. "You're not working hard at this like you used to."

Anna blinked back the tears, determined not to cry again, and told him all about Buddy and what had happened at the stables.

Pete whistled through his teeth and shook his head. "Tell me the name of this man again," he said, listening carefully and then typing the name into his cell phone. "We need to find a way to help both you *and* Buddy, and I think I know just what to do."

The following week, as Anna lay in bed with the bedroom door slightly open, she heard raised voices drifting up the stairs. Mom and Dad were arguing about something.

"I won't allow it!" Dad snapped. "The last thing she needs is to be reminded of all that."

"I disagree," Mom argued back. "It could be just what she needs to get over Buddy."

KEY WORDS

- go through
- enthusiasm
- blink back
- whistle

- slightly
- raised
- argue
- last

- disagree (↔ agree)
- get over

Get over Buddy? thought Anna. *But I don't want to "get over" him.*

She picked up the photograph and stroked the picture of Buddy's face. "Where are you now?" she murmured, "and what are you doing?"

There was a creak of floorboards on the landing, a tap at the door, and Josh's white face appeared.

"Can I come in?" he whispered. "I can't sleep with that row going on downstairs."

Anna beckoned him in, and he lay down on the bed beside her, snuggling up the way he used to do when he was little and scared of the dark.

"Will it help you to get better if I can find Buddy?" he murmured.

Anna's body tensed as she asked, "How will you do that?"

Josh shrugged and said, "I can go on my bike to that man's farm and see what's going on."

"No way!" said Anna. "It's too dangerous."

KEY WORDS

- creak
- floorboard
- landing
- tap
- row
- beckon
- beside

- snuggle up
- be scared of
- no way
- bedside table
- keyboard
- idly
- click

- scan
- specialize
- canned
- name
- supplier
- suddenly
- ingredient

Josh picked up Anna's tablet from her bedside table and tapped *J. Jackson & Co.* on the keyboard. Anna saw the same list of European meat companies that she had seen before. Josh idly clicked on one of them, and Anna scanned the information about a company that specialized in canned meat for pet food. *J. Jackson & Co.* was named as one of its suppliers.

Suddenly, Anna and Josh both gasped at the same time. The website showed a list of the ingredients that went into the pet food: chicken, beef, lamb… and horse meat.

The next morning was a Saturday, and Anna slept late. It had taken her hours to fall asleep, and when she did, her dreams were about Mr. Jackson chasing Buddy and Josh with a meat cleaver.

"Wake up, sleepyhead!" said Mom, with a smile. "Today we have a surprise for you, kindly arranged by Pete."

"But I thought Pete was busy at his new job," said Anna.

"He is busy. I think he is on duty later this afternoon. But still he really wants to help you. He thinks this will help you," said Mom.

Anna felt guilty that she had been thinking so much about Buddy that she hadn't asked Pete what his new job was. She decided that she would make up for it by asking him about it today, and wondered what kind of surprise he had arranged for her.

KEY WORDS

- **sleep late** (sleep-slept-slept)
- chase
- meat cleaver
- sleepyhead
- kindly
- arrange
- be on duty
- feel guilty
- decide
- make up for
- long for
- pull on
- drag
- hairbrush
- depend on
- intense
- conversation
- fist
- clench

By the time Anna was showered, dressed, and ready to leave the house, almost two hours had gone by.

She longed for the days when she could leap out of bed, pull on some clothes, drag a hairbrush through her hair and race outside. She hated having to depend on other people to do everything for her.

Josh was waiting outside by the car, holding onto his bicycle and having an intense conversation with Pete. Pete was frowning and shaking his head, his fists clenched.

Anna wondered what they were talking about, but when she approached, they leaped apart and put on fake smiles.

Pete helped Anna out of her wheelchair and into the car, his strong arms effortlessly lifting her as though she were a doll.

"What are you doing here?" she asked. "Are you coming with us to this surprise?"

"I was planning to come," said Pete, "but I'm afraid I can't, after all. Something important has come up, related to my new job, and I need to go and sort it out."

Mom and Dad looked as surprised as Anna felt, but they accepted Pete's explanation.

"Josh, get into the back of the car with Anna," said Dad, but Josh didn't move.

"I… er… promised that I would meet a friend," he said, his hands gripping the handlebars of his bicycle so tightly that his knuckles were white.

Dad frowned and looked at his watch. "We'll be back here in a couple of hours, so make sure that you're here too."

Josh glanced at Pete, and then nodded.

KEY WORDS

- accept
- explanation (*cf.* explain)
- handlebar
- knuckle
- a couple of hours
- glance at

Anna wondered what kind of surprise could possibly make her feel better, and her parents hadn't given her any clue about where they were going.

It was only when they turned into a large, clean stable yard that she realized where they were.

"This is Free Riders' Farm, the Riding for the Disabled place," she said, "but I'm not disabled. Does anyone even use that word these days?"

Mom turned in her seat and gave Anna a sympathetic look. "Disabled just means that you don't find it as easy to do things that other people might be able to."

"But doesn't it mean people in…?" Anna had been about to say "wheelchairs," and then she remembered that her own wheelchair was folded up in the trunk.

"Riding for the Disabled is a charity. Their activities are for anyone who needs some help and fun from horses so that they can enjoy life a bit more and maybe overcome some difficulties in their lives," explained Mom.

So that's it, thought Anna. *They think that I'm having some difficulty getting over Buddy and that I'll get better if I ride another horse.*

KEY WORDS

- possibly
- clue
- the disabled (*cf.* disabled)
- sympathetic
- be about to + *Verb*
- fold up (*cf.* folded)

- charity
- activity
- maybe
- overcome (overcome-overcame-overcome)
- that's it
- have difficulty + *Verb*-ing

Dad took her wheelchair from the trunk and lifted her into it, strapping her in like a baby so that she wouldn't tip out onto the ground.

A woman came striding across the yard, and Anna recognized the familiar blonde hair and the smile.

"Sally!" she called. "What are you doing here?"

"I got a job here after I had to leave the other stables," said Sally, crouching beside Anna's wheelchair, "and I'm going to help you get back on your feet."

"Do you know Pete, then?" asked Anna.

Sally blushed pink. "I met him when he came to the stables to have a look around and to arrange today's session for you. He seems like a nice guy."

Anna lifted her head and sniffed the air, enjoying the familiar scents of hay and horses. Perhaps this would be a good thing after all.

"Sally, I have to tell you something about Buddy," she began.

"No, Anna, I won't have you spreading rumors about Mr. Jackson when you have no evidence," ordered Dad. "I forbid it."

Anna's head dropped and she stared at her hands folded in her lap, feeling completely helpless.

Evidence — that's what she needed. But how would she get it?

POP QUIz

When did Sally first meet Pete?

ⓐ when she visited Anna at the hospital
ⓑ when Pete came to look around Free Riders' Farm

KEY WORDS

- tip
- blonde
- get a job
- crouch
- blush
- have a look around
- session
- sniff

- spread (spread-spread-spread)
- rumor
- evidence
- forbid (forbid-forbad(e)-forbid(den))
- stare at
- lap
- completely
- helpless

Free Riders' Farm had an indoor riding arena so that the horses could be ridden in all types of weather.

Anna sat in her wheelchair as Sally led out a small grey horse and made it stand still next to the mounting block, a heavy wooden block with steps cut into it.

"This is Lily," announced Sally. "She's the gentlest horse you will ever meet."

Anna held out a hand to feel Lily's soft, velvety nose and the warmth of her breath.

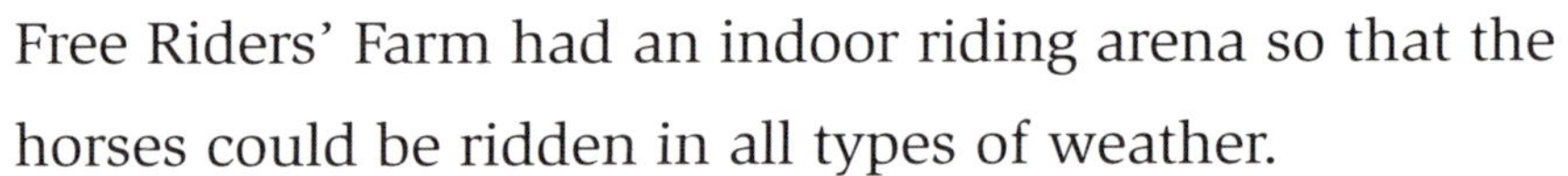

But something was wrong. Anna's hands felt sweaty yet cold
at the same time, and her heart was pounding hard. The
thought of actually sitting on Lily's back terrified her, and all
the memories of the accident with Buddy came rushing back
into her mind.

"I… I don't think I can do it," she whispered.

"Of course you can," said Sally. "Lily will take care of you,
and I'll be right here beside you. Don't worry, it's perfectly
normal to feel afraid after a nasty accident like the one you
had. You just need to get your confidence back."

Mark T for true or F for false.

Anna has never met Lily before.　　　T / F

KEY WORDS

- arena
- in all types of weather
- mounting block
- gentlest
- hold out

- velvety
- warmth
- sweaty (*cf.* sweat)
- terrify
- mind

- perfectly
- normal
- nasty
- confidence

Dad helped Anna out of the wheelchair, and he and Sally helped her onto the mounting block. She could only bear her weight on one leg, and had to lean hard on Dad's shoulder. Sally took Anna's leg in her gentle hands and slowly lifted it over Lily's back.

"You must tell me straight away if anything hurts," said Sally, anxiously.

Five minutes later, Anna was seated in Lily's saddle, her eyes squeezed shut and her fingers clinging tightly to the front of the saddle as Lily walked slowly around the arena.

"I'm going to fall," she gasped in panic.

"No, you're not," said Sally in a soothing voice.

But all Anna could think of was the sudden shock of a loud bang, Buddy rearing up onto his back legs, and the agony of the fall.

"I want to get off!" she said urgently. "Get me off!" She leaned forward and tugged at the reins, making Lily stop abruptly.

"Come on, honey," called Mom from the side of the arena. "You just need to push through the fear and everything will be all right."

But Anna was not going to push through the fear, and everything was *not* going to be all right. How could they all have forgotten Buddy so quickly?

KEY WORDS

- straight away
- anxiously
- be seated in
- shut (shut-shut-shut)

- cling (cling-clung-clung)
- soothing
- agony
- get off

- urgently
- tug at
- abruptly

"Bring the mounting block," she demanded, "and my wheelchair as well."

Lily seemed to sense that Anna was getting upset, and she shifted uncertainly, her ears flicking back and forward. Mom hurried over with the wheelchair, and Dad carried the heavy mounting block. Anna managed to slither down onto the block and then she collapsed into the wheelchair. Mom pushed her across the arena and back out into the yard.

"Leave me alone!" shouted Anna as soon as the wheels touched the smooth concrete of the stable yard. "I can wheel myself."

She seized hold of the large wheels and pushed down hard so that the wheelchair shot out of Mom's grasp. She heard Mom's startled cry, but she kept on going, and the last thing she heard as she wheeled herself around the corner was Sally's voice saying, "Let her go."

KEY WORDS

- as well
- sense
- get upset
- shift
- uncertainly
- slither
- as soon as

- wheel
- smooth
- concrete
- seize hold of
- grasp
- keep on + *Verb*-ing (keep-kept-kept)

FREE RIDERS'

A Fill in each blank with the right word below to complete each sentence.

> yard indoor block

❶ Riders could use the ______________ arena in all types of weather.

❷ Sally came striding across the ______________ to meet Anna when she arrived.

❸ Anna used a mounting ______________ to help her get onto Lily's back.

B Put the sentences in order.

❶ Sally helped Anna onto the mounting block.

❷ Sally gently lifted Anna's leg over Lily's back.

❸ Dad helped Anna out of her wheelchair.

❹ Anna leaned hard on Dad's shoulder.

________ → ________ → ________ → ________

 Choose the best answer to each question.

❶ Why did Anna and Josh gasp at the same time?

a) They heard Dad coming up the stairs.

b) They found that horse meat was used in pet food.

c) They realized that Pete had a surprise for Anna.

d) They thought that Mr. Jackson might chase them.

❷ Why did Anna panic when she was riding Lily?

a) She didn't believe that Lily was a gentle horse.

b) It reminded her of the accident with Buddy.

c) She couldn't remember how to make Lily stop.

d) There was a sudden loud bang.

❸ Why did Anna decide that everything was NOT going to be all right?

a) She thought that she would never walk again.

b) She thought that she would never ride a horse again.

c) She thought that everyone had forgotten about Buddy.

d) She thought that nobody cared about her.

Rescue

Anna's arms ached from wheeling the wheelchair; her leg hurt from sitting in Lily's saddle. But something inside her had changed — if nobody was going to help Buddy, then she would do it herself, no matter how difficult it was.

Her backpack hung on the handles of the wheelchair, with her medication, purse and cell phone in it.

With some difficulty and pain, she twisted around and managed to unhook it and pull it onto her lap. She pulled out her phone and rang the number for a local taxi company.

She had never needed a taxi before, and was a little nervous about using one, but she knew the number from an annoying advert that played on the radio every morning.

Once the taxi was booked, she wheeled herself cautiously back into the stable yard and looked around for the others. They were nowhere to be seen.

Anna guessed that they had gone back into the arena — to talk about her probably — and she hoped that they would stay there for a while.

As quickly as she could, she hurried across the yard, grateful that it was concrete and not rough dirt.

She waited at the entrance to Free Riders' Farm, at the edge of the road, hoping that passing traffic wouldn't knock her into the hedge.

How did Anna know the phone number for the taxi?
ⓐ from an advert
ⓑ from a phone book

KEY WORDS

- no matter how
- medication
- unhook
- **ring** (ring-rang-rung)
- the number
- annoying

- **advert** (= advertisement)
- play
- once
- book
- cautiously
- look around for

- grateful
- dirt
- entrance
- hedge

The taxi arrived quickly, driven by a cheerful man who looked old enough to be Anna's grandfather.

He looked surprised when he saw her. "Are you all right, Miss? I was expecting someone a bit older."

"I'm fine, thanks," said Anna, "but I may need some help getting out of the wheelchair."

"Oh, that's not a problem," said the taxi driver. "The roof is especially high so that you can stay in your wheelchair in the taxi."

He got out, humming a cheerful tune, and opened the back door. After releasing a ramp, he wheeled Anna into the taxi and fastened it to the floor with special bolts.

It reminded Anna uncomfortably of Buddy going up the ramp into Mr. Jackson's truck, and she had to shake her head to get rid of the memory.

KEY WORDS

- arrive
- cheerful
- expect
- hum
- tune
- fasten (↔ unfasten)
- bolt
- uncomfortably
- get rid of
- unload

It took about twenty minutes to reach the farm that was the address given on the Internet for *J. Jackson & Co*.

When Anna paid the taxi driver, he offered to wait, but Anna didn't know how long she would be there, so he unloaded Anna in the wheelchair, and he drove away.

Mr. Jackson's farm was a dirty, untidy kind of place. The fields were fenced in with rusty barbed wire and rotten wood. The lane that led up to it was overgrown with weeds, and there was an old, broken tractor abandoned halfway along it.

Anna found it almost impossible to wheel herself over the rough ground, and the sweat began to pour down her back. But she was determined to find Buddy and to get some evidence. If he *was* being badly treated, she would get some photographs on her phone. That would be enough evidence to show people.

And there was no time to waste. He could be taken away at any time to be made into… Anna couldn't bring herself to think about what might happen to him.

▲ barbed wire

▲ tractor

When she finally reached the farm yard, the stink of filthy stables made her nose itch.

A dog leaped out at her, barking and baring its teeth. Fortunately, it was chained to a wall and the chain was too short for the dog to reach her. Anna whispered to it, hoping that it would be quiet. If Mr. Jackson heard it, he would be out here in an instant. But there was no sign of a car or truck here, so hopefully he was out.

KEY WORDS

- untidy
- fence in
- rusty
- barbed wire
- rotten
- be overgrown with (*cf.* overgrow (overgrow - overgrew - overgrown))
- weed
- broken
- tractor
- halfway
- pour down
- waste
- be made into
- bring oneself to + *Verb*
- stink
- filthy
- bark
- bare
- be chained to (*cf.* chain)
- hopefully

Holding her breath, Anna wheeled herself across to the nearest stable. If she wheeled her chair up close and stretched up as tall as she could, she could just see over the top of the stable door.

She hardly recognized Buddy. His coat was dirty and had lost its shine, and he was so painfully thin that she could count his ribs. His hooves had grown long, and had curled up at the front. A thin discharge trickled from his nostrils and his sides heaved as he coughed.

"Buddy?" whispered Anna.

He didn't move. She struggled with the rusty bolt, and even when she did manage to slide it across, it was difficult to open the door with her wheelchair in the way.

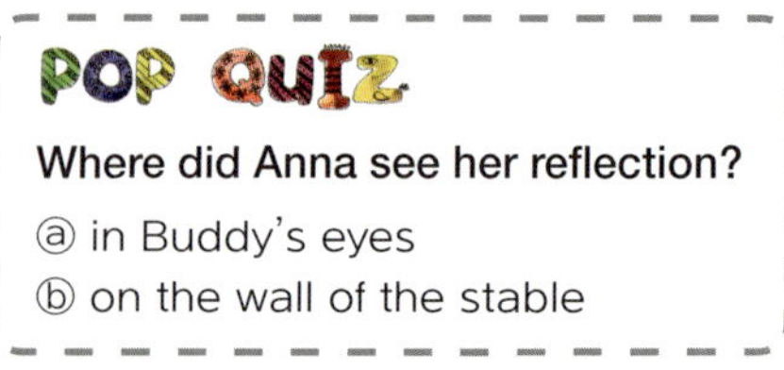

KEY WORDS

- hold one's breath
- nearest
- up close
- stretch
- painfully
- thin
- rib
- curl up
- discharge
- trickle
- heave
- in the way

At last, she managed to do it, and she wheeled her chair into the stable, wrinkling her nose at the smell.

"Buddy?" she murmured, laying a hand on his neck. The head collar he wore was too tight, and it had cut into the skin of his face, leaving sores. But at Anna's touch, he blinked and turned his head toward her so that she could see herself reflected in his weary eyes.

Just as she reached for her phone, Anna heard a sound that made her go cold. It was the sound of a truck engine, coming up the lane, closer and closer until, with the screech and hiss of its brakes, it pulled into the yard.

KEY WORDS

- sore
- **reflect** (*cf.* reflection)
- weary

- go cold
- screech
- hiss

- brake

A door slammed, and two pairs of footsteps strode across the yard, right towards Buddy's stable — one heavy and the other much lighter.  Mr. Jackson must have someone with him, which meant that Anna would be in twice as much trouble. What would he say when he discovered that she was hiding in his stable?

A shadow darkened the doorway and Anna shut her eyes,
waiting for the shouting to begin. Instead, there was a deep,
rich laugh. "Well, well, what do we have here?"
Anna opened her eyes to see Pete, the laughter fading as
he noticed Buddy's poor condition. Josh stood behind him,
watching anxiously.
"I'm not going to ask how you got here, Anna, or what you
were planning to do," Pete said. "Let's just get out of here
before Mr. Jackson comes back."
Anna wanted to hug them both, but she knew that they
didn't have much time. She wheeled herself out of the stable
and hugged Josh around the waist while Pete untied Buddy
and led him out into the yard.
He was still limping heavily on his bad leg, and his
overgrown hooves made it even more difficult for him to
walk.

KEY WORDS

- slam
- lighter
- be in trouble
- twice as much

- discover
- darken
- doorway
- laughter

- fade
- notice
- around the waist
- untie

"Anna, can you take Buddy while Josh and I lower the ramp?" asked Pete.

Anna nodded and, with a trembling hand, she took the rope as Buddy breathed his warm breath all over her and his ears pricked forward.

"Come on, Buddy, you can do this," said Anna, encouragingly.

But at that moment, the sound of another engine echoed around the yard, signaling that Mr. Jackson was back.

His truck roared into the yard in a cloud of exhaust fumes and he leaped from the cab, shaking his fist and swearing.

"What do you think you're doing, you thieves?" he yelled. "You have no right to take my property. I'm going to call the police."

KEY WORDS

- lower
- trembling
- prick
- encouragingly
- echo
- signal
- exhaust fumes
- swear
- thieves
- right
- property
- calmly
- officer
- documentary

"Actually," said Pete, calmly, "I *do* have the right to take your property, since I am an officer with the RSPCA."

Anna gasped — so Pete's new job was working for a charity that rescued animals! She had seen TV documentaries all about their work.

"It is illegal to keep animals in a state of neglect," Pete went on, "and I also have reason to believe that you are illegally trading in horse meat."

"But how did you know about that?" asked Anna astonished.

"I told him!" said Josh, jumping up and down with excitement behind Pete.

There was nothing Mr. Jackson could do but watch Buddy limp up the ramp and into the truck that Pete had hired.

Josh climbed into the cab and Pete lifted Anna up effortlessly with his big, strong arms. He put her wheelchair in the back with Buddy.

"Where are we taking him?" asked Anna.

Pete smiled. "I thought the people at Free Riders' Farm might take care of him. There's a very cute girl called Sally who works there, and I'm sure I can persuade her!"

He winked at Anna, who giggled.

Pete and Sally would make a great couple, she was sure.

KEY WORDS

- illegal (*cf.* illegally)
- a state of neglect (*cf.* neglect)
- trade in
- astonished
- but
- hire
- persuade
- wink
- giggle

Free Riders' Farm

Twenty minutes later, they arrived at Free Riders' Farm
to find Mom, Dad and Sally rushing around, frantically
searching for Anna.

"Thank goodness you're all right!" Mom said as Pete lifted
her out of the truck. "But what's going on? Why are you with
Pete, and what's Josh doing here?"

"He *was* meeting a friend," laughed Anna, "but not a human
friend."

Their faces looked astonished as Pete let down the ramp and
led Buddy down into the yard.

"Sally, would you do me a big favor and look after this poor
old boy for me?" he asked. "If you will, I'll take you out for
dinner."

POP QUIZ

What animal(s) already lived in the meadow?
ⓐ two donkeys
ⓑ a retired racehorse

KEY WORDS

- frantically
- thank goodness
- what's going on?
- do + *person* + a favour
- take + *person* + out
- meadow
- plenty of
- donkey
- beyond
- burst out laughing
- such a thing

Sally blushed bright red this time, and smiled into his eyes. "He can recover in the meadow where there's plenty of grass, and there are two old donkeys, too," she said, pointing toward a gate at the edge of the yard, with green grass beyond it. "I promise that he'll be safe here."

"And I'm sure we can help Buddy with that leg," Pete went on. "I have a friend who is a physical therapist for horses."

Josh burst out laughing. "I didn't know there was such a thing!" he said.

"But who will pay for it?" asked Anna.

"His new owner," said Pete, with a wink. "The RSPCA likes to find new homes for all their rescued animals."

"Another new owner?" said Anna, anxiously. "But who is it?"

Pete winked at her and said, "I did tell you that I wanted to have a horse of my own again…"

"It's you!" laughed Anna as relief flooded her body. "Can I take him to the meadow? Just Buddy and me together?"

Sally smiled and said, "Of course you can. You're a very brave girl, you know."

Mom and Dad wanted to stay and talk to Josh, to find out exactly what he had been doing, so nobody minded when Anna set off in the direction of the meadow.

She moved slowly, wheeling the chair with difficulty now. Her arms were exhausted and she felt limp after all the excitement.

But Buddy could only walk slowly anyway, and as the two of them made their way to the meadow, there was no need to say anything. They were together; they would both recover. And they would always be the best of friends.

KEY WORDS

▪ flood ▪ set off ▪ exhausted

Comprehension Quiz

A Mark T for true or F for false.

❶ The taxi driver expected Anna to be older than she was.　T　F

❷ Anna hugged Pete when she saw him.　T　F

❸ Mr. Jackson wanted to call the police.　T　F

❹ The RSPCA is a charity that rescues animals.　T　F

❺ Sally told Pete about the illegal horse meat trade.　T　F

B Fill in each blank with the right word below to complete each sentence.

sides	ribs	nostrils	hooves

❶ Buddy's ______________ heaved as he coughed.

❷ Buddy's ______________ had grown long, and had curled up at the front.

❸ Buddy's ______________ had a thin discharge coming from them.

❹ Buddy's ______________ were sticking out through his coat.

Choose the best answer to each question.

❶ Why did Anna find it difficult to recognize Buddy?

   a) His appearance had changed so much.

   b) It was such a long time since she had seen him.

   c) He was in a stable with several other similar horses.

   d) He was covered with mud.

❷ Why did Pete's laughter fade at Mr. Jackson's farm?

   a) He was angry that Anna was in the stable.

   b) He was worried that Josh would get into trouble.

   c) He was upset by Buddy's appearance.

   d) He was surprised that Mr. Jackson was not there.

❸ Why didn't Anna speak to Buddy on the way to the meadow?

   a) He didn't understand human speech.

   b) She couldn't think of anything to say.

   c) There was no need to say anything.

   d) They weren't friends anymore.

Let's Review the Story

Fill in the blanks to review the story.

Title: The Best of __________

Chapter 1: Anna loves horses. Her best friend is __________ . She is r__________ him when a loud noise startles him. He rears up and Anna is badly i__________ .

Chapter 2: Anna wakes up in the __________ . She is upset to learn that Buddy is also badly injured. Anna meets __________ , a physical __________ , who loves horses and is about to start a new job.

Chapter 3: When Anna goes to the __________ to say goodbye to Buddy, she sees him being taken away by Mr. __________ . She discovers that Mr. __________ has been c__________ to animals. She is worried about Buddy, but there seems to be n__________ she can do.

Chapter 4: Anna is horrified to discover that Mr. Jackson may also be an illegal horse __________ trader. Pete a__________ for Anna to try riding again at Free Riders' Farm. This experience reminds Anna of her __________ and she gets upset about Buddy. She decides to go to Mr. Jackson's farm alone, determined to take some photographs to provide __________ that he is cruel to animals.

Chapter 5: At Mr. Jackson's farm, Anna is shocked to discover that Buddy is in very p__________ condition. Pete and Josh come to help her r__________ Buddy, and when Mr. Jackson accuses Pete of being a thief, he reveals that he now works for an animal __________ and it is legal for him to take Buddy away. Buddy goes to a new home at Free Riders' Farm, where he and Anna can be __________ at last.

Let's Think & Talk

Think about the following questions and answer them freely.

❶ Buddy is Anna's best friend even though they can't talk with each other. Do you also have an animal friend like Buddy that understands you and comforts you even though it can't talk with you? Introduce the friend to us.
(If you don't have one now, what animal friend do you want to make? Tell us the animal and the reason.)

❷ Who is your best friend? Tell us why he or she is your best friend.

❸ Is there anyone who considers you as his or her best friend? What should you do to be someone's best friend?

❹ Search for organizations that protect animals internationally like the RSPCA and tell us what activities they perform.

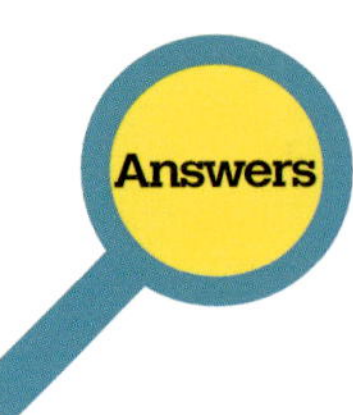

Let's Review the Story

Title: The Best of Friends

Chapter 1: Anna loves horses. Her best friend is **Buddy**. She is **riding** him when a loud noise startles him. He rears up and Anna is badly **injured**.

Chapter 2: Anna wakes up in the **hospital**. She is upset to learn that Buddy is also badly injured. Anna meets **Pete**, a physical **therapist**, who loves horses and is about to start a new job.

Chapter 3: When Anna goes to the **stables** to say goodbye to Buddy, she sees him being taken away by Mr. **Jackson**. She discovers that Mr. **Jackson** has been **cruel** to animals. She is worried about Buddy, but there seems to be **nothing** she can do.

Chapter 4: Anna is horrified to discover that Mr. Jackson may also be an illegal horse **meat** trader. Pete **arranges** for Anna to try riding again at Free Riders' Farm. This experience reminds Anna of her **accident** and she gets upset about Buddy. She decides to go to Mr. Jackson's farm alone, determined to take some photographs to provide **evidence** that he is cruel to animals.

Chapter 5: At Mr. Jackson's farm, Anna is shocked to discover that Buddy is in very **poor** condition. Pete and Josh come to help her **rescue** Buddy, and when Mr. Jackson accuses Pete of being a thief, he reveals that he now works for an animal **charity** and it is legal for him to take Buddy away. Buddy goes to a new home at Free Riders' Farm, where he and Anna can be **together** at last.

1. What does "obsess" mean?
   ① to think about one thing most of the time
   ② to act like an animal
   ③ to be happy about something
   ④ to get angry easily

2. What does "unfamiliar" mean?
   ① old   ② outdoor
   ③ not known   ④ dirty

3. Which of the following pair has the wrong past tense form of the verb?
   ① lie – lay   ② ride – rode
   ③ slide – slid   ④ spread – spred

※ Choose the right word for each blank. (4~5)

4.
   > The walls were covered ___________ pictures and posters of horses and ponies.

   ① into   ② with
   ③ toward   ④ through

5.
   > She hated having to depend ___________ other people.

   ① on   ② of
   ③ at   ④ with

※ Choose the common word for the two blanks. (6~7)

6.
> • You've got your riding lesson to look forward ______________.
> • Buddy doesn't belong ______________ us.

① of   ② to
③ in   ④ off

7.
> • Mom took hold ______________ Anna's hand again, shaking her head.
> • It said that Mr. Jackson had been accused ______________ animal cruelty.

① in   ② at
③ to   ④ of

8. Why did Josh think that computer games were better than horses?
Choose *two* answers.
  ① Computer games were cheaper to buy than horses.
  ② Computer games didn't poop everywhere.
  ③ Computer games didn't bite people.
  ④ Computer games didn't make clothes smell bad.

9. What shape was the outdoor school?
  ① a triangle   ② a rectangle
  ③ a circle   ④ a square

10. What are the rider's feet placed into?
  ① the bit   ② the girth
  ③ the reins   ④ the stirrups

11. What gave Anna the determination to wake up properly?

① Dad's voice

② the doctor's light

③ Mom's hug

④ Pete's exercises

12. Why didn't Mom go to the stables to see Buddy?

① She was scared of horses.

② She was too busy visiting Anna.

③ She didn't like Buddy.

④ She knew that the stables did not allow visitors.

13. Why was Pete going to leave the hospital?

① He was going to return to New Zealand.

② He was going to get married.

③ He was going to buy a new house.

④ He was going to start a new job.

14. Why didn't Dad want to drive Anna to the stables?

① He knew that Buddy was not there anymore.

② He thought that Anna should rest.

③ He did not want to spend money on more gas.

④ He did not know the way to the stables.

15. How did Anna find information about Mr. Jackson?

① She heard it on the radio.

② She read it in a book.

③ She saw it on a TV program.

④ She searched for it on the Internet.

16. **What was Mr. Jackson's punishment for treating his animals cruelly?**
Choose _two_ answers.
① He had to pay a large amount of money.
② His animals were taken away from him.
③ He was not allowed to keep any more animals for a year.
④ He was not allowed to keep animals ever again.

17. **Why hadn't Anna asked Pete about his new job?**
① She had been too busy thinking about Buddy.
② She thought that it might be rude to ask him.
③ She didn't want him to leave the hospital.
④ She hadn't seen him for a long time.

18. **What do you think Anna wanted to tell Sally?**
① that Pete was a nice guy
② that Buddy was in danger
③ that she was pleased that Pete had a new job
④ that she wanted to get on a horse again

19. **What made Anna's arms ache?**
① using the mounting block
② holding Lily's reins
③ carrying her backpack
④ wheeling herself in the wheelchair

20. **Why didn't the taxi driver wait at Mr. Jackson's farm for Anna?**
① She hadn't paid him any money.
② He had to pick up another passenger.
③ He didn't want to drive up the lane to the farm.
④ Anna didn't know how long she would be at the farm.

21. Why didn't the dog bite Anna at Mr. Jackson's farm?
① It was chained to a wall.
② It had no teeth.
③ It was calm and friendly.
④ It didn't see her.

22. What sound made Anna "go cold" at Mr. Jackson's farm?
① the dog barking
② Buddy coughing
③ someone speaking
④ a truck engine approaching

23. What did Mom and Dad want to talk to Josh about?
① his homework
② riding a bicycle safely
③ what he had been doing
④ what sort of job he wanted to do

※ Choose the wrong part of each sentence. (24~25)

24.
The people <u>who</u> <u>owned</u> the stables <u>always were</u> short <u>of</u> money.
    ① ②   ③   ④

25.
<u>Important</u> something has <u>come</u> up, <u>related</u> <u>to</u> my new job.
  ①   ②   ③ ④

26. What are the correct words for the blank?

① will she   ② won't she
③ does she   ④ doesn't she

27. What is the correct sentence?
① Anna squeezed her legs to let him know that it was time to walk.
② Anna squeezed her legs to let him to know it was time walking.
③ Anna squeezed her legs to let him to know that it was time walk.
④ Anna squeezed her legs to let him know that it was time walking.

Sarah J. Dodd

Sarah J. Dodd is an experienced primary school teacher who resides in the UK, but has also lived and taught in Australia. She has a PhD in Science and a certificate in Creative Writing. She has published several books for children: "An Angel Anyway" (Anyway Press, 2008) the "Little Angels" series (Lion Children's Books, 2009/10), "The Lion Picture Bible" (Lion Children's Books, 2015) and "Legs: the tale of a meerkat lost and found" (Lion Children's Books, 2015). Her poetry for children has also been highly commended and published in the anthology "Let in the Stars" (Manchester Metropolitan University, 2014).
She is currently working on further picture books for the very young, and a novel for older children.

The Best of Friends

Written by Sarah J. Dodd
Illustrated by Cloi

First Published in May 2016

Editorial Manager: Juyon Choi
Editors: Kyunghee Jang, Jiyeong Park
Designers: Eunhee Lee, Elim
Cover Designer: Eunhee Lee

Published and distributed by

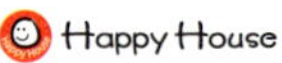

Darakwon Bldg., 64-1 Jandari-ro, Mapo-gu, Seoul, Korea 04031
Tel: 82-2-736-2031(ext. 250)   Fax: 82-2-732-2037
Homepage: www.ihappyhouse.co.kr
Publisher: Kyudo Chung

ISBN: 978-89-6653-405-0 18740 / 978-89-6653-156-1 18740(set)

[Components]
• 1 Audio CD (Recording Studio: Aram)
• Answer Keys & Korean Translation: Free download at www.ihappyhouse.co.kr